CONTENTS

INTRODUCTION

The Easter season is one of the most wonderful times of the year—a special, annual celebration that features an exciting, and sometimes strange, mixture of the secular and sacred. Nowhere else on the calendar can you find a holiday that blends an ancient Roman crucifixion with chocolate bunnies, an empty tomb with egg hunts and enough pastel colors to make an Ivy League preppy blush.

Yet there is a uniquely beautiful sanctity to this holiday that isn't found at any other time of the year. For Christians, no day is as hallowed as Easter Sunday because of what it represents. Like a springtime herald, Easter proclaims anew each year the death and resurrection of God's Son, Jesus Christ, whose great sacrifice provides salvation to all who trust in him for the forgiveness of their sins. The Easter message is the heart of the gospel.

For churches, there is perhaps no better opportunity than Easter to reach a dark, dying world with this life-changing good news. Statistics show that most churches won't see the same increased attendance figures again until the following spring. Easter is not only a distinctively meaningful occasion to remind believers of the hope they have in the resurrection; it's also literally a once-a-year chance to share the good news of Jesus with countless unbelievers who might never step foot in a church otherwise.

That's where *The Hope of Easter* Church Kit comes in. This kit is specially designed to help your church push past the secular trappings of the holiday and celebrate the true Hope of Easter, the Savior who died for lost sinners and rose again so that they might have eternal life. By using this kit, your church will be able to share that hope with the community around you and make your service an extra-special experience that both members and guests will remember. The kit contains everything you need to plan and host a powerful Easter service based on the theme of Jesus as the Hope of Easter. This includes practical resources for reaching out to your community and promoting the service, and even a complete sermon to relieve the pressure as you plan a spiritually impactful morning.

One of the most valuable pieces of *The Hope of Easter* is a gift book that you can provide for church members and visitors to help make their Easter celebrations more meaningful than ever. Filled with gospel truth, this book takes readers on an exciting journey through history to explore the origins of Easter, its connection to Scripture, God's plan of salvation through his Son, the veracity of Jesus's resurrection, and why the empty tomb provides incredible spiritual hope to every believer both now and for the life to come. The book is designed to be engaging, accessible, and uplifting for both long-time believers and those new to Christianity. What's more, the book will serve as a tangible bridge for readers between your one-time Easter service and continued spiritual growth in the days to come.

Easter offers an incredible opportunity for your church to reach the lost and encourage Christians to rejoice and grow in the eternal hope that is already theirs in Christ. Jesus's death and resurrection provide amazing blessings—salvation from sins and righteousness before God—that aren't available anywhere else. May *The Hope of Easter* be a tool that opens hearts and minds to receive those gifts this Easter.

GETTING STARTED

The Hope of Easter Church Kit gives you the tools and insights you need to host a powerful Easter service full of hope and truth. For many churches, Easter is by far the most attended service of the year, providing exclusive opportunities to draw the church family together and reach out to the local community. As you plan your Easter service, we've included the following suggestions to help your church make the most of this one-of-a-kind morning.

- Begin with prayer. Ask God to use *The Hope of Easter* to speak to you, your leadership team, your church members, and visitors in powerful ways.

- Read over all of the materials in the Church Kit and make notes about what you think will work best for your church.

- Plan your Easter service. Read through the sermon provided in the kit, plan to show the Welcome Video at the start of the service, explore music that supports the truths of Easter (e.g. hope, sacrifice, atonement, resurrection, salvation, forgiveness, victory, new life, etc.), decide what messages and announcements you want to share, determine who will be involved in the service, and plan for special parts of the service, such as communion and a specific gospel call.

- Present the service details and the overall promotion of *The Hope of Easter* concept to your leadership team and ask them for insights and suggestions.

- Schedule a time to speak to small group leaders and present the materials to them. Ask for their input about what will benefit their group members, as well as how they'd like to be involved in supporting the community outreach.

- Schedule a kick-off date to begin promoting your Easter service using your roadside marquee sign, church bulletin, website, and social media sites.

- Show the Promotional and Invitation Videos included in the kit to your entire congregation and ask them to invite friends and family to attend the Easter service.

- Collect comments from small groups and members of your congregation, asking them to share what Easter means to them, and how they'd like to see *The Hope of Easter* affect your church the rest of the year.

WHAT'S INSIDE THE CHURCH KIT

This Church Kit includes everything you need to plan and lead a meaningful and memorable *Hope of Easter* service on Resurrection Sunday.

Church Kit Digital Resources DVD

The Digital Resources DVD includes all of the digital content you need:

- **Easter Invitation Video:** Remind your congregation to invite their family, friends, neighbors, and coworkers to church during the season with this invitation video. Show it during the weeks leading up to your Easter service. It's also great for sharing on social media and your website.

- **Promotional Video:** Show this video in the weeks leading up to your service to get your members excited and planning to attend.

- **Countdown Video:** Play it before the service begins.

- **Easter Service Welcome Video:** Show this video at the start of your service to help the congregation prepare to celebrate and worship together.

- **PowerPoint Template:** Customize these slides to use throughout your service while carrying the design and theme of *The Hope of Easter*.

- **Bulletin Insert Template:** This file enables you to create and print 5.5" by 8.5" inserts for your church bulletin. The bulletin insert is designed so that you can easily add text for announcements, sign-ups, or sermon notes.

- **Web and Social Media Graphics:** This folder features banners and buttons you can use on your website and social media platforms to help promote your *Hope of Easter* service with attractive and consistent visuals.

The Hope of Easter Sermon

The Church Kit contains a complete sermon to be given on Easter Sunday. The message is provided as a resource for the pastor or church leader to use as-is or to adapt and personalize. The sermon gives a biblical definition of hope and expounds on why Jesus's death and resurrection provide life-changing hope not only for this life, but the life to come. Furthermore, it calls both believers and seekers to respond to the hope found in the cross and the empty tomb.

The Hope of Easter Gift Book

This book is designed as a gift to be given to both church members and visitors. You may want to order and distribute them early in the Easter season, as well as have plenty on hand to give as gifts to every family at your Easter service. This book is a powerful reminder of the hope that Jesus's resurrection provides now and into eternity.

Sample Invitational Tools

Get a firsthand look at some of the resources you can use to promote your service. See the Resource Flyer for more information on invitational tools like direct mail postcards, DoorHangers, posters, banners, and more. This kit includes a few samples of these tools.

STEPS FOR SUCCESS

STEP 1: PLAN

A great Easter Sunday service begins with prayer and planning, and this section of the guide helps you think through the planning steps and schedule for your *Hope of Easter* service.

1. Pray. Begin by asking God to direct and inspire your plans for *The Hope of Easter* service and to start moving in the hearts of your members so they will be open to God's call to worship this Easter season.

2. Read. Read through *The Hope of Easter* gift book, the sermon, and the files on the Digital Resources DVD. Then watch the videos and review the Resource Flyer and the sample invitational tools and books.

3. Cast the Vision. Before launching the planning phase of *The Hope of Easter,* meet with your leadership team and cast a vision for how you believe this service will affect your church and your community. Consider using these methods for creating a shared vision:

- Show *The Hope of Easter* Promotional Video to your team.
- Read a portion of *The Hope of Easter* gift book to engage people in preparing their hearts and minds for the Easter season.
- Pray together for the success of your service.
- Pass around samples of *The Hope of Easter* materials from the Church Kit.

4. Engage Your Leaders. Many of your church's ministries will be affected by *The Hope of Easter* service, so plan to meet with all of your ministry leaders to ask for their help and support. One of the keys to a great campaign is focus. Keep your ministries working together and supporting the overall goals of the church.

- **Small Groups:** If you plan to invite visitors and church members to sign up for small groups after *The Hope of Easter* service, make sure to talk with your small group leaders in advance. Encourage your leaders to develop a short, simple explanation of their small group and its purpose. You may want to ask small group leaders to put together a listing of small groups that are available to send out to people who attended your *Hope of Easter* service. Be sure your leaders plan for new members and are prepared to smoothly integrate them into their groups. You may even want to do a training session for your leaders and talk with them about how to welcome new people and help them feel comfortable in a new church setting.

- **Parking, Greeters, and Ushers:** The logistics of getting a family to church on Easter Sunday can be overwhelming. The experience people have getting *to* your service may be the most important part of helping them have a meaningful experience *in* your service. It's crucial to plan for additional people and recruit plenty of volunteers. Start in advance and encourage your church members to make it a family event to volunteer and welcome guests to your church. You may want to establish a logistics team to focus on traffic, parking, and seating. Another hospitality team can focus on welcoming people and providing information, possibly food/drink, and even small gifts. Easter Sunday may be the only time many families attend a church service with their kids. Providing coloring sheets and crayons or other small activities for children when they walk in the door can help families feel welcome and comfortable. While these things seem secondary to the important message of Jesus's resurrection, they are vital to making people feel comfortable and open to hearing the message of *The Hope of Easter* service.

- **Children's Ministry:** Since you will have new families visiting your church, you should plan on welcoming more children into your children's ministry and nursery rooms. Talk with ministry leaders about lesson plans, visitor gifts, information packets for visiting parents, and childcare volunteer requirements. See the "Step 3: Host" section for more information.

- **Assimilation:** Talk with your assimilation team about plans to follow up with visitors through phone calls, e-mails, and letters.

- **Prayer:** Encourage your prayer team to pray for the service and all the outreach plans.

5. Create a Detailed Plan. Use the Event Planning Template on the Resources DVD to create a detailed plan and schedule that includes action steps, owners, and deadlines.

6. Get What You Need. Review the materials in this kit, and then order the invitational tools, banners, and resources you need for your church members at Outreach.com/HopeofEaster.

7. Order Gift Books. *The Hope of Easter* gift book makes an excellent gift and follow-up tool for your church members and visitors. Decide how you will distribute them and order plenty of copies to give out during the Easter service. You may want to order them far enough in advance to have a team of people wrap them in ribbon to set them apart as a special Easter gift from your church to each family.

STEP 2: PROMOTE

1. Start Early. Begin promoting *The Hope of Easter* service at least four weeks before Easter Sunday. You'll want to make sure both the church family and the community know about your service so they can make their Easter plans ahead of time.

2. Cast a Vision for Your Congregation. Good leaders are critical to the success of any effort. Most members of a congregation rise only as high as the expectations set by their leaders, so cast a vision of complete participation. Consider the leadership principles and vision-casting exhibited by Nehemiah:

Then I said to them, "You see the trouble we are in: Jerusalem lies in ruins, and its gates have been burned with fire. Come, let us rebuild the wall of Jerusalem, and we will no longer be in disgrace." I also told them about the gracious hand of my God on me and what the king had said to me. They replied, "Let us start rebuilding." So they began this good work. (Nehemiah 2:17-18, NIV)

Good leaders cast a vision for what the group can do together that they can't do as well on their own. Ask everyone to pray for the success of the service and outreach efforts—and for personal growth and richer worship during the Easter season.

3. Send Invitations. Use creative ideas and high-quality communication tools to reach out to your community!

- Use a direct mail postcard to tell your community about your *Hope of Easter* service. Visit Outreach.com or call an Outreach Specialist at 1-800-991-6011 for assistance in planning a direct mail campaign.

- Hang an eye-catching *The Hope of Easter* banner outside your church to attract people passing by. Remember to include your service times and either a phone number or web address.

- Organize volunteers to distribute *The Hope of Easter* Door-Hangers in the neighborhoods closest to your church.

4. Get the Church on Board. Get your members excited about Easter Sunday and inviting new people to your church. Share some of the details about the service and follow-up events. Also, ask for additional volunteers to act as greeters, childcare helpers, ushers, parking lot attendants, and hosts.

- Include information about *The Hope of Easter* in your church newsletter and in the announcements during your weekend services leading up to Easter.

- Use a Connection Card or *The Hope of Easter* bulletin insert to create a volunteer sign-up for the service and events.

- Let the congregation know this will be a special, unique Sunday. Encourage everyone to make time in their schedule to attend and to invite at least one friend or family member to the service.

- Send an e-mail to your congregation. Share your vision and plans for *The Hope of Easter* service and encourage everyone to take part.

- Show the Promotional Video and the Invitation Video during Sunday services on the four Sundays before Easter to be sure everyone knows about and gets excited to be part of *The Hope of Easter* service.

5. Equip Your Members to Be Inviters.

- Use the Bulletin Insert Template on the Digital Resources DVD to create a *Hope of Easter* prayer list. Include three to five blank lines, and ask your members to list friends and church ministries they will support in prayer. Make this list available to all who will commit to praying; you might mention it in your bulletin three to four weeks before Easter.

- Help your members extend successful invitations by providing themed DoorHangers or postcards to invite friends, neighbors, and co-workers to your service.

6. Get Online. Place a banner or button on your church's home page and create a web page about *The Hope of Easter*. Web images are available on the Digital Resources DVD.

7. Maximize Social Networks. Announce *The Hope of Easter* Sunday service and any follow-up events on your Facebook, Instagram, Pinterest, and other pages. Create a Facebook event, and ask each church member to like, share, and comment on the page. Encourage them to post photos of their preparations for Easter. Use other social media sites as appropriate, and see the Social Media Handbook on the Digital Resources DVD.

8. Tweet and Text. Send announcements through your church Twitter feed, or enlist volunteers to do this. Ask members to re-tweet. You can also send suggested text and web links for church members to use to invite friends to your service. Example: *Taking the whole family to the #HopeofEaster service on Easter Sunday. Who wants to join us?*

9. Post on Community Calendars. Contact newspapers, TV and radio stations, local magazines, mail-out coupon flyers, recreation centers, and clubs—anyone who posts a calendar of events. Make sure they have the times, location, and other important information about your *Hope of Easter* service.

10. Get on the Air and in Print. Ask local radio stations and newspapers to promote your Easter service. Develop a press release for local news outlets (see the Press Release Template on the Digital Resources DVD).

PROMOTIONAL TOOLS

SEE THE RESOURCE FLYER FOR MORE INFORMATION

STEP 3: HOST

1. Get Your Members Involved. An Easter service requires the teamwork of many people, so make sure your members know how they can get involved.

- **Invite Ministry Leaders to Participate in the Service.** Introducing ministry leaders is just one way people can find out about opportunities to get involved in the church beyond Easter.

- **Host a Ministry Fair.** Using God-given gifts is an act of worship and obedience. Be sure to include each ministry in the church: Nursery, Children's Church, Visitation, Small Groups, Worship Team, and more. Ask ministry leaders to prepare handouts to give to those who are interested.

- **Use Bulletin Inserts.** The Digital Resources DVD contains a Bulletin Insert Template. Make a list of the ministries available in your church and include the leaders' names and contact information.

- **PowerPoint Slides.** Highlight one or two ministries using the PowerPoint Templates included on the Digital Resources DVD.

- **Social Media.** Encourage ministry leaders to blog or participate on your church's Facebook page and other social media sites.

2. Get Ready for Visitors. Not only is *The Hope of Easter* service a time to energize your congregation for the Easter season, it's also a time to welcome new families into the church and reach out to the community in meaningful ways. People are often open to an invitation to an Easter service even though they wouldn't attend a regular service. Let your regular church attendees know that their participation is valuable and appreciated.

- **Create a Welcoming Atmosphere.** Encourage regular attendees (whether they are official volunteers or not) to greet visitors and help them find the nursery, children's ministry rooms, and even the restrooms. Encourage your congregation to watch for people who may be alone on Easter Sunday and invite them to sit with them and join them for refreshments after the service.

- **Give Visitors a Welcome Packet.** Welcome packets can include a pen and paper, a coupon to the church coffee kiosk, or a magnet with contact information and the church web address. The goal is to encourage visitors to learn more about your church.

- **Invite Visitors to Return.** This sounds simple, but issuing a clear invitation to return and become part of your church family is an important way to make visitors feel valued and welcome.

- **Connect Visitors to a Small Group or Sunday School Class.** New people will be more likely to keep attending if they can make a friend or two and quickly feel like they belong. Small groups or Sunday school classes are a great way to facilitate this connection. While you don't want visitors on Easter to feel pressured into attending, you do want them to feel welcome and to have the information they need to make the choice to get involved with your church beyond *The Hope of Easter* service.

- **Serve Refreshments.** After the service, have a clearly marked area with drinks and snacks. Not only does this demonstrate that you value your attendees and their experience, but it also encourages everyone to stay for a while and meet new people.

STEP 4: CONNECT

The overall goal for *The Hope of Easter* campaign is to help people experience the life-changing power of the gospel on Easter Sunday and beyond. Church is where we gather to worship collectively—through music, study, service, and more—and where we receive spiritual edification. Offer church members and visitors opportunities to connect both inside and outside the church to experience and continue *The Hope of Easter* in their own lives.

- **Host a Ministry and Event Fair.** As previously mentioned, a ministry fair is a fun way to introduce families to the various opportunities to experience *The Hope of Easter* in their lives throughout the year.

- **Create Family-Centered Events.** *The Hope of Easter* is not contained to just Resurrection Sunday. There are many opportunities both before and after Easter to create family-centered events. Let people know that you love their families and want to keep them connected to your church through fun, meaningful events.

- **Set Up a Care Committee.** Let families know whom to call when they're facing an emergency. Do they need babysitting? Meals prepared? Help moving? Let your members know they can get in touch with a care committee member and get help from their church family. Help each other worship through suffering and hard times by supporting and serving each other.

NEXT STEPS

While *The Hope of Easter* service is a one-time event, it is also a starting place for so much more. It is an opportunity to purposefully welcome members and guests to join you in the privilege of worshipping the risen Savior. As you lead your congregation in meditating on the death, burial, and resurrection of Jesus, you will help attendees experience the redemptive power of the empty tomb, which can transform people for eternity.

However your church engages the community during this wonderful season of remembrance and worship, *The Hope of Easter* is intended to be an inspirational and memorable celebration. Use it to supplement and add creativity. Take the ideas and activities and adapt them as you see fit to help your church rejoice in what the Lord has accomplished for all believers through Christ. We hope the resources you find here will help you and your church exalt and worship the crucified and risen Son of God!

OUTREACH®

Outreach Inc., Colorado Springs, CO 80919

Outreach.com

PLANNING GUIDE

The HOPE of EASTER

HOW TO MAKE THE MOST OF YOUR EASTER SUNDAY SERVICE